Making Mead

BRYAN ACTON & PETER DUNCAN

– a complete guide to the making of sweet and dry Mead, Melomel, Metheglin, Hippocras, Pyment and Cyser

Amateur Winemaker

Published by

G.W. Kent, Inc.
3691 Morgan Road
Ann Arbor, Michigan
48108 U.S.A.

© Argus Books Ltd. 1984

Sixteenth Impression 1985
Reprinted 1987
Reprinted 1990
ISBN 0 900841 07 9

Printed in U.S.A.

Contents

Illustrations

Pictures by: Radio Times Hulton Picture Library, C. Green, L. Dyer.

The Honey Bee at work.

Preface

Mead, as everyone knows, is a pleasant, alcoholic drink made by fermenting honey and water with yeast.

Of all the crafts of mankind, mead-making is almost certainly the oldest. It is likely that mead was made even before the wheel was invented. Cave paintings of primitive stone-age men depict the collection of honey from bee colonies, and any addition of water to this would automatically produce a mixture which could be fermented by wild yeasts. The discovery of alcohol almost certainly occurred in this chance manner, and spread to all parts of the world.

The method of making mead remained almost unchanged for thousands of years until fairly recently when advanced mead-makers such as Brother Adam of Buckfast Abbey and Mr C. B. Dennis published informative pamphlets outlining the basic principles of mead-making. This book is a further extension of their work by introducing people to melomels as well as mead. Melomels (fermented honey and fruit juices) utilise less honey per gallon than mead, and we believe that once the delicate flavour of honey is appreciated in these drinks people will be moved to make mead once more in appreciable quantity.

Whereas most mead-makers are at present apiarists, we are writing mainly for the non-beekeeping fraternity, who are as much entitled to their mead as were their ancestors in Elizabethan, Anglo-Saxon or Celtic Britain.

A glass of lightly chilled mead on a summer's evening, when one is at peace, is a splendid thing. On a cold winter's night, a hot spiced pyment is a re-discovery of a delight that "Mr Pickwick" took as a matter of course.

Compared with wine prices, a bottle of mead is cheapness itself. At 12–14% alcohol by volume it is stronger than most table wines and quite as delicious – especially when it is your own!

We hope that you, on reading this book, will be inspired to join us in this admirable craft which has an end-product which stimulates, invigorates and satisfies man's most desired aim – Contentment.

G. W. B. Acton & P. M. Duncan.

Man's Oldest Drink

Among the multitude of things which constitute the daily life of mankind through all the ages, certain things have always been accorded a special place of importance. Basic elements such as air, fire and water formed the groundwork of primitive science and also of magic, while commodities, such things as salt, wine, bread and honey were woven into the myths, folk-lore and religions of every race at every time in history.

The bee is such an amazing creature that it is hardly surprising that honey (and mead also) became attributed with the most remarkable of properties. Honey was for thousands of years the principal sweetening agent known to mankind; honey and mead were the givers of life, wisdom, courage and strength right from the earliest history, through Hindu times, on through Aristotle and Virgil until they found powerful echoes in the Bible. Even our own Celtic ancestors made mead and a form of metheglin by mixing honey with the juice of the hazel tree which was to them a magic tree. Some of the Saints (particularly the Irish ones) were partial to a drop of mead. St Findian, who lived on bread and water all week, used to eat salmon and drink mead on Sundays (a precedent if anyone asks what is the best wine to serve with salmon). That great Irish saint, St Brigitte, went one step further and merits consideration as the patron saint of amateur winemakers. Once when the King of Leinster visited her they ran out of drink, and St Brigitte took a great vat of water and turned it into mead, thereby emulating Christ's miracle at Cana. It is unfortunate that she did not leave her recipe for this "Instant Mead".

In later times, mead tended to decline somewhat. Beekeepers still made mead, and good mead, as many of them do today, but fashions tended to change. On the one hand there grew up a whole range of metheglins (made by fermenting honey and spices or by steeping spices in mead), many of which were intended purely as medicines, and on the other hand court circles indulged themselves in ever more complicated "pyments".

In Elizabethan times, when drinking standards reached their lowest ebb, hundreds of recipes for different "pyments" were in circulation. These "pyments" were not true pyments made from fermenting grape juice and honey, but were concoctions of mead with spices, syrups, grape wines and many odd substances. Already sweet meads were sweetened further, and so many spices were added to some that the bouquet must have been rather like after-shave lotion.

Queen Elizabeth's own royal recipe for mead has survived to this day, although no winemaker in his senses would want to make such a sickly concoction. We have, however, included a modern adaption of it which will prove most satisfactory insofar as the herbs (for it is really a metheglin) are infused in the finished mead. This enables the winemaker to exercise more control over how much herb flavour is imparted to the drink.

Among ordinary people, however, mead became two drinks. It still continued as a wine, generally for special occasions and particularly weddings. Most people know that the word "honeymoon" comes from the practice of drinking honey wines during the month-long celebrations which followed better class weddings, but not everyone knows that in some parts it was the custom to pack the bride off to bed and then fill up the bridegroom with mead until he could not stand. At this point, he was carried to bed alongside his bride and it was common belief that he would then sire a son that very night. If, by chance, the bride did conceive and bear a son nine months later, the maker of the mead was complimented upon its quality.

We moderns call any drink made from honey "mead", but apart from being a wine, mead was also a beer or ale. The Anglo-Saxon word for mead was "alu", significantly close to "ale", and almost certainly the mead which the Vikings drank so copiously was more of a beer than a wine. Undoubtedly, there was an ale-like drink made from honey during the Napoleonic wars, since trouble occurred in the British Army when the alcoholic strength of mead supplied to the troops was reduced from 6% to 4%. This is definitely ale strength, and mead was in fact made with hops and was fermented with a brewers' yeast. In most inns, ale and mead were sold side by side along with cider.

Until the 18th century, of course, sugar was not used by the great mass of the population; it was so expensive that it could be afforded only by royalty and the wealthiest. Honey was the common sweetener, and it was therefore honey which was used to make the common people's drinks. It was only with the opening up of the West Indies and the creation of plantations of sugar cane with slave labour in the 18th century that bulk supplies of sugar for Europe became available, bringing its price down and putting it within everyone's reach. Supplies were further assured by the discovery of beet sugar by Napoleon's scientists in their efforts to beat the British blockade during the Napoleonic wars. Thereafter sugar gradually supplanted honey as the popular sweetener.

As honey slipped out of favour so, inevitably, did wines and beers made from it; as beer brewing became more and more organised, so malt beer became cheaper to produce than mead. The flavour of ale did not differ very much from that of low alcohol meads, so that from then on mead declined very rapidly as a staple drink in this country.

Wine type meads and melomels and metheglins survived, of course, and formed the basic amateur winemaking of those days, which we now inherit. In our recipes we have included an ale-type one as a curiosity. It is certainly a genuine old-time drink, but would probably be regarded with blank astonishment if it were entered in a mead class at the National Honey Show.

———— • ————

At Gulval, near Penzance, Cornwall, there used to be held the ancient ceremony of "blessing the mead". The mead festival was held on St Bartholomew's Day (24th August) since, down to the Middle Ages, St Bartholomew was the patron saint of the honey crop and was therefore associated with mead-making. Here the blessed mead is being poured into one of the vats in the Mead House, where mead was once made commercially.

Meads, Maids and Marriage

In our researches into mead's history we have occasionally come across material which really is suitable for a more light-hearted article, and some stories which are far too robust for modern publication.

We made a start on Nordic mythology, since we knew that mead played a very big part indeed in Norse legends. The Norse gods were a reckless, wild-living lot, much given to blatant venery. Episode after episode arose in which one god would give some goddess a few draughts of mead, following which her resistance would be visibly reduced so that the scheming god, like a Victorian villain, would enjoy her physical delights with impunity. Suttung's daughter Gunnlod was particularly prone to this form of seduction, and indeed appeared to thrive on it, for on one occasion, when Odin stole the mead from Suttung (not knowing how to make it himself) Gunnlod was overcome with grief since Odin had someone else in mind at that particular time. Later, however, she turned the tables on Odin by giving *him* a few draughts of mead so that he became like clay in her hands. He remarked, as he slowly went under from the aphrodisiac qualities of mead, that it gave him the gift of poetry and of composition (the authors will refrain from commenting on what is inspiring their prose at the moment).

Returning home from the British Museum with our heads full of these Norse legends, and eyeing our mead with a sideways look, we resolved to turn to the non-mythological, very real world of the ancient Hindus. Alas, it was much the same story, less colourful perhaps, and portrayed in a more refined manner. In those days honey was believed to be some form of magical dew which dropped from heaven and was collected by the bees. In one of the Sanskrit hymns, known collectively as the Rig-vedas, it states: "In the

11

wide-striding Vishnu's highest footsteps there is a Spring of Mead." This spring, it was believed, made people very fertile, and young girls, betrothed to some intended husband, were well plied with mead so that they would honour their families by giving birth to a son within a year of marriage.

When we came to study the Greek civilisation we had already guessed what would be found, for we knew that old roisterer Bacchus had been the God of Mead long before he became accepted as the God of Wine. Virgil and Homer wrote about mead in glowing terms, as they did about ambrosia, which was apparently a semi-solid mead liqueur of ancient times and reputed to be the food of the Gods.

The Greek civilisation was unique and has never since been rivalled. Basically, the Greeks maintained a splendid balance amongst all aspects of life. Love, parenthood, respect for the law, love of their gods and family life were all kept in harmony, and by some subtle trick of the mind they were able to explore any one avenue of life without it interferring in any way with any other aspect. There were no frustrations, repressions or guilt feelings among the Greeks. Sardanapalus, the last king of Assyria, summed it up well in his words: "I have been a king, and as long as my eyes have seen the light of the sun, I have eaten, drunk and done homage to the joys of love, knowing that the lifetime of men is short and subject to much change and misfortune." Mead, of course, was what they drank, and it was offered as a sacrifice to the goddess Aphrodite by ladies of good brewing, that they might get "a good bag of lovers".

Naturally, the Greeks had other pleasures too. Thus, there appears to have been a definite mead-making season, and the mead would be matured and kept for an orgy, called a Dionysia (from Dionysus, the God's other name), which took place once or twice a year. On these occasions the lightly-clad ladies and the men in their goat-skins would climb to the summit of a not-too-high mountain and then proceed, very methodically, to get "tight" on their mead, whereupon they would perform dances and make sacrifices which very quickly became orgies (the details of which we must spare your tired eyes). The customs they practised were really quite remarkable, and they attributed this entirely to the influence of the mead, which was not, apparently, drunk at any

12

other time of the year (at least, not in any quantity).

Despite their debauchery, they frowned upon anything which struck them as inelegant, and poor old Hippocleides, for instance, was severely censured by his father on his wedding night, when, having drunk too much mead, he insisted on standing on his head, stark naked, on the dining table and waving his legs in the air while he sang a merry song. For this bit of naughtiness his father refused to let him take his bride.

Having recovered from the Greeks, and decided that our mead stock had better be kept under lock and key, we turned to the Moorish civilisation. It was not long, however, before we reached the phrase "The Moors considered honey to be a love-stimulant." Indeed, Beck and Smedley remark that Moorish wedding celebrations were really sex-orgies at which the guests were given honey and honey-wines until they were drunk because they believed these contained powerful aphrodisiacal ingredients.

In Roman times we come across Pollio Romulus writing to Julius Caesar about it. Pollio was over 100 years of age and apparently (if he was not boasting) enjoyed a full sexual life. This he attributed to drinking copiously of the local Welsh metheglin and to rubbing his legs with "oyl".

Nearer home, in the 17th century, Sir Kenelm Digby quotes: "The Meathe (Mead) is singularly good for a consumption, stone, gravel, weak-sight, and many more things. A chief burgomaster of Antwerp used for many years to drink no other drink than this and though he were an old man, he was of extraordinary vigour, had always a great appetite, good digestion and had *every year a child*".

In a very British way we might say "Ah well! There's no telling what these foreigners get up to", but an examination of our own history reveals much the same erotic story though the emphasis is more on the ability to stay the course rather than on mead's stimulating effect on the imagination. That is probably why the Scots have a saying that mead-drinkers have as much strength as meat-eaters.

We have only quoted a small proportion of the references linking mead with sex, but they suffice to show that this belief was not only world-wide but covered all periods of man's history. Professor Jung once marked that if one finds a belief in several unconnected cultures at different times in history, one should be

13

wary of dismissing it out of hand. The evidence of centenarians enjoying "the full life" is even less easily brushed aside.

Some scientists have attempted to belittle the virtues of mead and honey by analysing their chemical constituents and showing that carrots or other edibles are richer in this or that substance. Fortunately, this attempt to mislead is being refuted by other scientists and doctors who are discovering that honey and mead are, in fact, valuable invigorating and revitalising aids, particularly when we live in an age of processed foods.

As to its qualities as a sexual stimulant, while it was certainly the principal aphrodisiac in ancient times, we must remember that people in those days tended to drink more heavily than we do. Certainly no family catastrophe could possibly result from giving your great-aunt an occasional glass of mead, and for those mead-makers determined on having a long life and a gay one, we would remind them not to forget the castor oil (to rub on their legs, of course!).

Honeys for Mead

Modern researchers confirm that the bees which produce our honeys have one of the most highly organised social systems in the insect world.

To give some idea of its wonder, one need only consider the curious "Dance of the Bees". This is in fact a complex method of conveying information about sources of food outside the hive. When bees are feeding on a rich source of food, small white glandular patches on their abdomens are exposed, and it would appear that some kind of scent is emitted, so that a "beacon" is left for later bees. When the bee returns to the hive it does a sort of dance at the entrance to the hive or on a honey comb. For example, if the source of food is less than about 100 yards from the hive, the bees perform a circular dance first one way and then the other. This type of dance acts as a signal to other worker bees who stream off in all directions from the hive, to quarter the immediate neighbourhood and locate the scent "beacon" signalling the source of food. As more and more bees eventually find the food source, the "beacon" effect becomes stronger so that later bees emerging from the hive are able to fly directly to the supply, a very important factor since a worker bee's lifespan is mainly dependent upon how long its wings last.

If the food source is more than about 100 yards from the hive, the returning bee performs a figure of eight dance and wags its abdomen on the straight part of its run. It has been found that the farther away is the source of food, the slower the dance is performed but that more wags of the tail were performed in each sequence. The great research worker in this field, Von Frisch, discovered that from the time taken over the dance and the number of wags it was possible to calculate fairly closely the distance of the food source from the hive. In addition, the bee's body during the straight part of the dance actually points towards the source of the food (to within a few degrees). The dance is only performed when the sun is shining or when there is at least one patch of clear blue sky. It would appear from this and other evidence that bees are sensitive to the polarised light which comes from blue sky and which permits them to locate the position of the sun, thereby enabling them to indicate direction even when the sun itself is obscured. The whole process is a beautiful piece of time and motion study which bees have been doing for ages before mankind ever came to organise itself in as efficient a manner.

Honey is made from the nectar of flowers, and is named according to the type of blossom from which the nectar is collected by the bees.

If you ask a British bee-keeper which type of honey is best for making mead, he will generally reply that any sort is good as long as it comes from these islands of ours. It would be folly to contradict him lest he call on his legions of bees to drive one from his land, yet, since we are concerned with the truth and not with British solidarity in this matter, it is necessary to consider the point from a different angle. It is possible in theory to obtain honey from any kind of blossom. As a matter of fact, while the nectar of most blossoms is wholesome, even from most poisonous plants, there are a few plants whose nectar is toxic to man. Rhododendron nectar has long been under suspicion in this respect, and cases do occur from time to time of people suffering ill-effects from eating one of these rare honeys. Such instances are, of course, very infrequent, and if one buys, say, Guatemalan Wild Honey it will certainly be quite sound and wholesome.

The collection of honey by bees is not a continuous process, for it is influenced by weather conditions, particularly by blue skies and by the relative humidity. Comparatively little honey is produced during the Spring, since flowers are relatively scarce and many sorties over long distances are often needed to obtain enough nectar to provide the bee colony with its daily requirements of food. This is why Spring blossom honeys are almost unknown in this country, although in Mediterranean climates such as that of Spain, so much honey is collected in the very short hot Spring that there is an immediate surplus which finds its way into our shops as Spanish Orange blossom honey or Acacia blossom honey.

16

In this country, summer is the time when the greatest quantity of honey is made. During June, July and August, the bees are collecting nectar whenever weather conditions allow, and sometimes quite astonishing quantities are brought back to the hive in the space of a few days. Some types of flowers surrender their nectar much more freely than others, and someone once worked out that it would take seventeen miles of normal garden border to equal the yield from a single acre of clover. Clover and heather (also known as ling) are the two largest single sources of nectar in Britain. It is the honey from these flowers which comprises the principal type produced and sold by many British bee-keepers.

In other countries, where the honey glut occurs at different times of the year, the emphasis is elsewhere, so that a great variety of honeys are obtainable, such as orange blossom, acacia blossom, lime, rose, rosemary, as well as curiosities such as leatherwood honey from New Zealand.

Most English apiarists will affirm that English honey has more flavour in it than foreign honeys, and a simple test of buying some honeys and tasting them will generally prove that this is true. By and large, English honey is full-flavoured while foreign honeys are usually somewhat milder.

Most mead-makers (who, at present, are mainly bee-keepers) will also assert that because heather honey is our most full-flavoured honey it will also make the best mead. We are not bee-keepers and have no allegiances to maintain in that direction, and we must take issue on this point very strongly. Mead in its matured state is very much like a good white wine, and as such may reasonably be expected to reach full maturity within two or three years. As it happens, heather honey imparts such a strong flavour to mead that it tastes unbalanced unless it is matured for perhaps as long as eight years.

Undoubtedly heather mead so matured is excellent beyond words, but this zealous devotion to heather honey has given birth to the idea that all meads require such lengthy maturing. Such a belief has for years bedevilled the winemaking world and has prevented a great many winemakers from trying their hand at mead-making.

The way round this impasse is to use more delicately flavoured honeys or to use heather honey in smaller quantities mixed with fruit juices in melomels. Under these conditions meads and melomels mature as early as do white fruit wines, and we have even tasted some good meads (one a first prize winner at a big show) that were only a few months old.

In our view, the finest meads are made from single-blossom honeys, and of these, clover, acacia, orange, rose, wild-rose and rosemary are outstanding.

They are easily obtainable from most stores these days, although if one can obtain English clover honey direct from a bee-keeper it is worth the slight extra expense. The reason is, of course, that such honey is fresh and, in common with other winemaking ingredients, will produce better mead because none of its delicacy has been lost during storage.

Mixed blossom honeys rank next as mead-makers, but the mead does not have quite the same character and its flavour will generally prove poorer than that obtained from single-blossom honey.

Below these honeys we place heather (or ling) honey, for the reasons already stated. It is entirely a matter of the time element. If you are a patient winemaker and can wait eight years, then put heather honey up near the top of your list, but not otherwise.

Most of the honey sold in shops does not fall into any of the categories just mentioned. It is labelled "Blended" and often in small type one can see that other things have been added to the honey so that it will spread better on bread and so on. These blended honeys are really of little use for making mead since the product will lack character. Such honeys, however, are useful when making melomels and metheglins if cost is important, since the honey plays a lesser part in these drinks. There are many excellent Australian honeys, both single blossom and blended, but one needs to guard against the admittedly rare chance of purchasing eucalyptus blossom honey, which has a peculiar but typical bitter flavour. Most Australian honeys, it should be emphasised, are entirely satisfactory. So, too, is New Zealand honey, indeed it is in most respects very similar to our own native honey.

Honey from such countries as Mexico, Jamaica, Guatemala and Rumania often have an advantage in that they are less pure than honey from Britain, Canada or the U.S.A. The eternal quest for purer and purer honey is not in our view a symbol of advancement but rather the opposite. One sometimes overhears bee-keepers commenting on the problem of pollen clogging their filters when purifying it. They seem blind to the fact that it is many of these so-called "impurities" in honey which give it its bouquet and flavour.

Some honey is light in colour and some dark. With a few exceptions the darker honey is more strongly flavoured and in consequence, since most meads are delicate light wines, it follows that the lighter and milder honeys are usually more suitable. For melomels, metheglins, pyments and hippocras, however, darker and stronger honeys may sometimes be preferable, although this is by no means generally applicable.

One feature of honey often causes confusion. Honey may be obtained either in a liquid or a crystalline state, and the question as to which form should be used and how much is required is commonly raised. Since solid honey is formed simply by the crystallisation of the liquid variety, the two types should be, and generally are, essentially identical. This can easily be proved by dissolving 450 g (1 lb) of each type in 1.1 l (2 pt) of water and bringing the volume up to 2.25 l (½ gal) when both solutions will have the same gravity or nearly so. The difference between the two is generally so small that it can be quite safely ignored. It is only when crystallisation is accompanied by simultaneous loss of water that significant differences between the two forms of honey begin to become apparent. Such occurrences are fortunately relatively rare, but we have encountered one example where a 20% difference in gravity was observed. Hence, to avoid any chance of errors arising from exceptional honeys of this nature, it is probably better though certainly not essential to adjust mead musts to a predetermined initial gravity rather than work solely on the basis of a given weight of honey.

To sum up: good mead demands good honey. At the time of writing, mead is made by bee-keepers and by few others. Even here, many bee-keepers value their honey and beeswax above their mead. The reason is that mead is often made from the honey trapped in the wax so that combs are simply soaked in water and this product then fermented. This is all wrong! As our good friend Mr S. W. Andrews, that well-known bee-keeper and winemaker, one said: "If you want the best mead, you must use your best honey!"

Mead-making Technique

Having obtained your honey, you will be wanting to begin operations, so let us discuss basic mead-making procedure.

During fermentation the yeast, which is a type of fungus, acts on the sugar in the "must" (the liquid to be fermented) and splits it into carbon dioxide and alcohol together with a small amount of energy which it uses for its growth and reproduction. As well as sugar, however, yeast also needs certain nutrients, mainly nitrogenous substances, to keep it healthy, in much the same manner as we need vitamins. Yeast does have one great advantage over us – it can live in the absence of air and does so when fermenting mead musts. Its source of energy is sugar, and it will continue to thrive in a sugary solution in the absence of air until the by-products of its own metabolism, alcohol in this case, become too concentrated and kill it off. Fermentation then ceases and no more alcohol is produced. Fortunately, the wine yeasts now on the market can tolerate fairly large amounts of alcohol and will normally not become inhibited until 15% or more alcohol by volume has been produced.

Hence, all the winemaker has to do is to co-operate with the yeast so that it has ideal conditions in which to work, and to ensure that no other organism is allowed to enter in quantity to disrupt the yeast colony.

There follows a series of basic rules which every mead-maker should observe, although it is unfortunately impossible in a book of this size to relate the reasons which lie behind all the points mentioned. If, however, they are all followed, there should be no cause for dissatisfaction even in the very first mead or melomel made.

This is all you will need in the way of equipment for making a gallon or so of mead: a saucepan for boiling, a plastic bucket, a tube of some sort for siphoning, a glass one-gallon fermenting jar, fitted with a fermentation lock, a fine sieve or straining cloths, a plastic funnel, and a wooden or stainless steel spoon. Most of this can be found in the average kitchen, but it will also be useful to have the other things shown – a hydrometer and jar, wine yeast, yeast nutrient, Campden tablets, and sulphite solution.

BASIC RULES

Preparation of the Must

(*a*) Sterilise the honey and water mixture with sulphite or by boiling, although the latter method is definitely likely to lead to a poorer mead.

(*b*) Adjust the mixture (must) with acid and tannin as per recipe.

(*c*) Ensure a plentiful supply of nutrients.

(*d*) Add the yeast at the correct temperature.

Fermentation

(*a*) Keep the fermentation container at the correct temperature (*see* page 24).

(*b*) Keep the container covered or fitted with a fermentation lock at all times except when actually inspecting or adjusting the fermentation.

(*c*) Add additional honey (if required) as the yeast can absorb it, dissolving the honey in a little of the must before adding it to the bulk, and stirring well.

(*d*) Do not ferment in metal containers (plastic buckets or glass containers are best).

Later Care

(*a*) Rack (i.e. siphon) the mead off the yeast carefully so that as little as possible of the sediment is sucked up.

(*b*) Top up the maturing jar with tap water if necessary so that no large air space is left in the jar. It is a good idea to make a few pints extra for topping up purposes to avoid dilution in this manner.

(*c*) Fit the jar with an air-lock.

(*d*) Add one Campden tablet per 4.5 l (1 gal) at each racking.

(*e*) Subsequent rackings should be made at 3–4 month intervals and should be conducted without much splashing.

General

(*a*) Keep all equipment clean and sterile.

Honey and water alone represent a very poorly-balanced "must", which is why meads made from these two ingredients alone ferment very slowly and mature rather poorly; such mead requires perhaps eight years before it is drinkable. There is no need to mature mead for so long if the must is first adjusted to conform to the basic rules of modern mead-making.

In order to obtain a sound fermentation and a finely flavoured product, it is necessary that a must should contain the following:

Good quality honey.
Water.
Acid.
Yeast nutrients.
Tannin.

In addition, a good yeast is required.

Honey has already been discussed in detail, so let us consider the other items of this ideal must.

WATER

In general winemaking, there are often enough trace elements present in the ingredients to offset any deficiency in the local water supply. Where, however, honey is the sole ingredient, the question of trace elements becomes of paramount importance. Most of the water supply of this country contains a fair amount of trace elements except, perhaps, magnesium. We have found by experiment that, if a must is made with distilled water instead of tap-water, the fermentation will very quickly "stick" and the only thing which will revive the yeast into activity is a pinch of Epsom Salts (Magnesium sulphate). It is well worth remembering this fact when dealing with mead musts if there are no magnesium salts in your local water supply.

ACID

Acids play a big part in fermentation, and, indeed, on the final flavour of the mead. Where a must is deficient in acid, certain peculiarly flavoured substances are produced during fermentation and these spoil the finished mead. It tastes more like cough-mixture than mead! Since honey and water form a solution with a very low buffer capacity in comparison with normal wine musts, however, small amounts of acid have a very significant influence which is much more apparent with meads than with other wines. Indeed, mead is about the only wine where some correlation between titratable acidity and pH can be observed and the latter does give a fairly reliable indication of its acidity and acid taste (provided it be measured accurately). In consequence, meads require a lower acidity than other wines and should preferably contain no more than about 2.5–3.5 parts per thousand acid (in terms of sulphuric acid standard) with 3.0 ppt being a good average value. Pure mead musts therefore need only 15–20 g (½–¾ oz) acid per 4.5 l (1 gal). On the other hand, melomels and other similar honey drinks (except metheglins) should be treated as normal wines with respect to acidity.

The type of acid used in mead-making is rather important. Citric acid has always been the standard additive in mead-making and many mead-makers like the flavour it imparts. Nevertheless, it is not the best acid to use if superior meads are sought. The best acid combination is ⅔ malic acid and ⅓ tartaric acid (Mead acid mixture).

Various older publications on mead generally include a formula which is an acid plus nutrient mixture. This formula is of very ancient origin and is very suitable for old-style meads of the ale type. It is, however, not so suitable for modern wine-type meads and we have therefore not included it.

NUTRIENTS

The main nutrient for the yeast required in mead-making is ammonium phosphate. It can be obtained in 250 gm jars (½ lb approx) quite cheaply through chemists or in the form of yeast nutrient tablets from amateur winemaking suppliers. One level teaspoonful of ammonium phosphate or 2 nutrient tablets is sufficient for a gallon of mead must.

Vitamin B_1 is also advisable to ensure a thriving yeast colony and this can either be added in tablet form (one 5 mgm tablet per 9 l (two gallons)) or as the proprietary food Marmite (¼ teaspoonful per 4.5 l (1 gal)).

We have already mentioned the advisability of adding a pinch of Epsom Salts (Magnesium sulphate) per 4.5 l (1 gal) (1 gm per 4.5 litres exact measurement) in case of any deficiency in the local water supply, but in addition, in an ideal mead must a small amount of potassium phosphate (nutrient) should also be added (2 gms or ¼ teaspoonful per 4.5 l (1 gal)).

TANNIN

Meads that lack astringency lack character. In old-style meads this astringency was imparted either by adding hops or by adding herbs as in metheglins. Tannin is the main source of astringency in wines and we recommend this to be added to meads preferably in the form of grape tannin or tannic acid (¹⁄₁₅–¹⁄₂₀th oz per 4.5 l (1 gal)).

Having discussed the main additives for mead, we become aware of the differing needs of novices and advanced mead-makers. Ideally, beginners would start off as advanced mead-makers and adjust their musts with a mixture of acids and other chemicals to produce a balanced must. In practice, we realise that many mead-makers still rely on the hit-and-miss method of using the juice of two lemons for acid adjustment and a tablespoonful of cold tea for astringency. Since we cannot change the world in a single day, we give below two alternative mixtures which are required in the must in addition to the honey and water. These are, of course, for straight meads only, and where melomels, metheglins, pyments, hippocras or cyser are contemplated it is better to rely on the recipe. We must nevertheless confess to being reluctant to advise the use of lemons and cold tea since many mead-makers fail to achieve a consistently high average standard of quality because they are unwilling to adopt more refined techniques. The reader is therefore urged to slough this habit as soon as possible if his or her aim is to make better mead.

Beginners' additives (per 4.5 l (1 gal))

Juice of two lemons
¼ teaspoonful of Marmite.
Pinch of Epsom Salts.
1 teaspoonful Ammonium phosphate (or 2 nutrient tablets).
1 tablespoonful of very strong tea.

Advanced mead-maker's additives (per 4.5 l (1 gal))

5 gms Ammonium phosphate.
2 gms Potassium phosphate.
1 gm Magnesium sulphate.   } nutrients
1 5-milligram Vitamin B_1 tablet per 9 l (2 gals).
2 gms Tannic acid.
6.5 gms Tartaric acid.
10.5 gms Malic acid.
3.5 gms Citric acid.

In view of the difficulty of measuring out such small quantities, it is sometimes better to multiply these quantities by 20 (other than the vitamin tablet which is best added separately), obtain this quantity from a chemist made up to 1.1 l (2 pt) with distilled water, whereupon it is only necessary to measure out 60 ml (2 fl oz) of the mixture in a kitchen measure to obtain the correct amount of acid and nutrients for 4.5 l (1 gal) of mead. If the solution is kept in a tightly sealed bottle in the refrigerator it should keep quite well and the 1.1 l (2 pt) provides all the acid/tannin/nutrient requirements for 90 litres (20 gals) of mead.

YEAST

Brewer's yeast is only suitable for producing ale-like meads in vogue during Napoleonic times and earlier. It is of no use at all in producing wine-meads.

Baker's yeast is a little better, but it cannot be recommended as the delicate flavour of the mead is easily overcome by the off-flavours imparted once baker's yeast starts to die and autolyse.

A yeast which has often been recommended for mead-making is Maury yeast. It is difficult to see why, since it is a rather slow fermenting yeast and the flocculent sediment is easily disturbed, making racking more difficult.

Tokay yeast is a flocculent yeast which, however, does lend itself well to mead-making. Our friend Mr E. A. Roycroft tells us that he has had considerable success with it. The secret appears to be that this yeast requires a fermentation temperature of 35°C (95°F) which is abnormally high by winemaking standards.

Sedimentary white wine yeasts are, for the average mead-maker, the best ones to employ. The principal varieties used for meads and melomels are: Sauternes, Bordeaux, Steinberg, Bernkastler, Zeltinger, Champagne, Liebfraumilch, Graves and General Purpose (this latter yeast is generally a variation of a white wine yeast). Each type has its devotees, and we would not presume to rate one much above the others in quality, but only in its ability, given the right conditions, to produce a slight variation in the flavour of the finished mead. We do have our own preferences for Steinberg and Sauternes, however, and would recommend these to novices inexperienced with wine-yeasts.

TEMPERATURE

For most wine yeasts, a fermentation should ideally commence at about 26°C (78°F), drop to about 18°C (65°F) during most of the fermentation and be completed at about 27°C (80°F). This ensures that the fermentation gets off to a good start and avoids contamination from other organisms. The main fermentation is leisurely and avoids dissipation of the flavouring constituents by their being volatalised and thereby lost in the stream of carbon dioxide evolved during the fermentation. The final temperature of 27°C (80°F) ensures that all residual sugar is metabolised leaving the mead perfectly dry (sweetening-up if required, occurs later when the mead is stable). Such ideal conditions are rarely possible and for most purposes fermentation at 21–24°C (70–75°F) will prove quite satisfactory.

THE HYDROMETER

Readers will notice that here and there in the recipes we refer to certain operations being carried out at "Gravity 5" or "Gravity 0" and may wonder to what these refer. These are actually hydrometer readings, "Gravity 5" being 1.005 and "Gravity 0" being 1.000.

Let us make it quite clear that a hydrometer is not essential to mead-making, and it is probable that the majority of present mead-makers do not in fact use one. They rely upon years of experience in judging the volume of carbon dioxide bubbles and the taste of the fermenting must to gauge the point at which to add more honey (if required) or at which to rack. The advantage of the hydrometer is that it achieves the same objective without the need for years of experience at making mead. Thus, in this respect, the beginner who uses a hydrometer gains an advantage of several years over another beginner who does not.

The hydrometer has many uses which are fully outlined in another book in this series – "First Steps in Winemaking" (£2.00, postage 71p) and instructions as to its use are included with every one sold. Hydrometers are obtainable from most winemaking suppliers and cost about £2.00 together with a test or trial jar.

For the beginner who does not at present have a hydrometer we would offer this piece of advice. A fermenting mead or melomel should not have any further honey added nor should it be racked until it is "dry" or nearly so except when a sweet wine is desired. Precaution must then be taken to ensure that it is stabilised so that no further fermentation can occur.

The fermentation of meads is usually slow, but we have tried to remedy this to some extent by adding nutrients and acid to the basic honey and water. It also requires fairly lengthy maturing in order to achieve its optimum quality. As such, it is worthwhile making the occasional gallon of mead for storage, and to fill the gap by making melomels which ferment much more quickly and may be drunk much earlier.

BASIC PROCEDURE

1. Prepare must as directed in the recipe.
2. Allow fermentation to proceed to completion unless otherwise stated.
3. Rack within a week of fermentation finishing, taking care to avoid too much aeration. Add 50 ppm sulphite (1 Campden

tablet per 4.5 litres (1 gal)).

4. Rack a second time as soon as a heavy deposit forms or after 3 months, whichever is the sooner, and add 50 ppm sulphite.
5. Rack again every 3–4 months, sulphiting 50 ppm every second racking (or every racking if preferred).
6. Mature until the wine is at its peak of perfection, i.e. 1–3 years for light meads and longer for fuller types. Most meads may be drunk much sooner, but adequate maturing is essential if superior wines are desired. Maturing in cask is advisable only if quantities larger than about 45 litres (10 gals) are contemplated otherwise too much oxidation may occur.

Using the standard hydrometer.

MEAD RECIPES

RECIPE No. 1 – DRY MEAD

Ingredients:

1.3 kg (3 lb) Clover honey
10 g (¼ oz) Tartaric acid
15 g (½ oz) Malic acid
Water to 4.5 litres (1 gal)

Nutrients
Steinberg yeast
¹⁄₁₅th oz Tannin

Method:

Dissolve the honey in 2 litres (½ gal) warm water together with the nutrients, acid and tannin. Make the volume up to 4.5 litres (1 gal) with cold water and add 100 ppm sulphite. After 24 hours add the yeast starter and allow to ferment to dryness. Thereafter proceed as recommended in the text.

RECIPE No. 2 – DRY MEAD

Ingredients:

1.1 kg (2½ lb) Acacia blossom Honey
10 g (¼ oz) Tartaric acid
15 g (½ oz) Malic acid
Water to 4.5 litres (1 gal)

Nutrients
Champagne yeast
¹⁄₂₀th oz Tannin

Method:

Proceed exactly as directed in the previous recipe. This mead can be made into a sparkling wine if desired and is an excellent wine for blending in a cuvee for sparkling wine production. (See Champagne chapter of "Making Wines Like Those You Buy" in this series.)

RECIPE No. 3 – LIGHT SWEET MEAD

Ingredients:

1.3 kg (3 lb) Orange blossom Honey
10 g (¼ oz) Tartaric acid
15 g (½ oz) Malic acid
Water to 4.5 litres (1 gal)

Nutrients
Sauternes yeast
¹⁄₁₅th oz Tannin

Method:
Proceed exactly as described in the previous recipes but rack for the first time when the gravity drops to 20. Rack again at a gravity of 15 and if fermentation resumes once more rack for a third time at a gravity of 12. Thereafter mature in the normal manner, racking carefully every 3–4 months. This procedure will give a sweet mead whose alcoholic strength is around 12% by volume.

RECIPE No. 4 – SWEET MEAD

Ingredients:

Acacia blossom Honey as required　　**Nutrients**
10 g (¼ oz) Tartaric acid　　　　　　**Madeira yeast**
15 g (½ oz) Malic acid　　　　　　　**¹⁄₁₅th oz Tannin**
Water to 4.5 litres (1 gal)

Method:
Prepare the must exactly as before, using 1.3 kg (3 lb) honey. Ferment until the gravity drops to 5 then add 110 g (¼ lb) honey per gallon, making sure that the increment of honey is thoroughly dissolved. Repeat the procedure whenever the gravity drops to 5 until fermentation finally ceases and then rack. Thereafter proceed as recommended in the text.

RECIPE No. 5 – SWEET MEAD

Method:
Proceed exactly as in Recipe No. 4 except that heather honey should be used instead of acacia blossom honey. The resultant mead will be much stronger in flavour and require considerable maturing. Even then, it does not appeal to everyone!

RECIPE No. 6 – QUEEN ELIZABETH'S MEAD

Ingredients:

1.3 kg (3 lb) Heather Honey　　　**Nutrients**
10 g (¼ oz) Tartaric acid　　　　　**Madeira yeast**
15 g (½ oz) Malic acid　　　　　　**¹⁄₁₅th oz Tannin**
Water to 4.5 litres (1 gal)
Herbs as detailed below

Method:
Dissolve the honey, acid, tannin and nutrients in 2.85 l (5 pt) warm water, then add 1.1 l (2 pt) cold water and 100 ppm sulphite (2 Campden tablets). After 24 hours add the yeast starter and thereafter proceed as directed in the basic procedure. After the wine is 3–6 months old, suspend in it a muslin bag containing 15 g (½ oz) Rosemary 15 g (½ oz) bay leaves, 15 g (½ oz) thyme and 10 g (¼ oz) sweet briar. Taste the wine daily until the flavour extracted from the herbs appears satisfactory, then remove the bag of herbs. The wine should then be matured for at least another 6 months, and may possibly require fining in order to clear any haze produced by the herbs.

RECIPE No. 7 – ALE MEAD

Ingredients:

450 g (1 lb) Honey (preferably English)	**Nutrients**
30 g (1 oz) Hops	**Brewers yeast**
10 g (¼ oz) Citric acid	**Water to 4.5 litres (1 gal)**

Method:
Dissolve the honey in 3.5 l (6 pt) hot water and bring to the boil. Add the hops and boil vigorously for about 45 minutes. A few of the hops should not be added initially but put in about 5 minutes before the "wort" reaches the end of the boiling period. Strain off the hops, add the citric acid and nutrients, allow to cool overnight (covered closely) then make volume to 4.5 l (1 gal) with cold water. Add the yeast to the cool wort and allow to ferment to completion, skimming off the yeast daily as for beer. Allow to settle for a few days after fermentation ceases, then rack into quart beer bottles adding one level teaspoonful of sugar to each bottle. Stopper the bottles firmly, store in a warm place for 2–3 days to ensure bottle fermentation begins then move into a cooler location to assist clarification. Subsequently treat as a bottled beer. Priming is not, of course, essential and after fermentation the ale mead may be matured as a draught beer and drunk after a few months.

Racking a jar of finished mead into clean bottles.

Melomels

There is in every one of us a deep-seated desire to return to our primitive state. At one pole of this desire are such evils as outbreaks of mob violence, but on a more cultured level are such things as the great satisfaction felt by a city dweller, used to central heating, when he sits by a countryman's open log fire. With these thoughts in mind, one might have expected that among winemakers there would have been a basic yearning to make mead, like their ancestors, having mastered the elementary techniques of general winemaking. It may be that such a yearning does exist, but despite the fact that mead has played a gigantic part in our history, much greater than that of wine, beer and spirits lumped together, mead-making has been on the decline for centuries. Only in countries such as Ethiopia is it still the national drink. The reason is, of course, the high cost of honey, a problem which is not new since a high price merely reflects scarcity, and nearly always in the world's history there was insufficient honey to make the mead required by the expanding populations. Today, the gap is filled with other beverages, but in former times ingenuity had to express itself in other ways. Some honey was always reserved for the mead needed for religious ceremonies, but the rest was "stretched out" by mixing it with fruit juices to make honey wines known as melomels.

Some melomels so dominated a region that they acquired particular names of their own. The most famous was Pyment, made from grape juice and honey, although the term "pyment" later represented a whole series of drinks of many different types. Another one was Cyser, made from apple juice and honey.

The big advantage of melomels is that they retain the character of mead to a large extent, and utilise much less honey than meads, so that they are hardly more expensive to produce than ordinary wines. Moreover, fermentation is much speedier than is usually the case with meads. Melomels can in fact be produced and matured more or less as are fruit wines of the same type.

Unfortunately, not every type of fruit juice makes a pleasant melomel when fermented with honey. The high tannin of many red fruits causes a distinct clash on the palate when its astringency is mixed with the flavour of honey. For this reason, the winemaker is advised not to make elderberry melomel or blackberry melomel. Some case can be made out for an elderberry melomel if only the juice is used without severe pressing, but otherwise this fruit is best reserved for general winemaking. The principal dark coloured fruits which do blend well with honey are redcurrants and blackcurrants, and these melomels have proved popular for centuries in some parts of the country under the names of Red Mead and Black Mead.

To place melomels correctly in the winemaker's repertoire it is best to think of them in terms of light white wines, and to treat their production with the extreme care that is required to produce good white wines.

Almost any form of white fruit can be employed successfully, e.g. apricots, peaches, gooseberries, greengages, the paler type of cherries and rhubarb as well as canned juices such as pineapple, orange, passionfruit and grapefruit. The latter juice, indeed, can be made into an aperitif melomel of exquisite character.

Whereas in mead production the quality of the honey is paramount, this is not so important when making melomels, although a few types of blended honeys, such as Australian honey if made from eucalyptus nectar or U.S.A. honey when it is over-processed, are best avoided.

The question of sterilising the honey becomes important at this point. Honey contains a great many impurities from the winemaking point of view, principally wild yeasts, vinegar bacteria and other hostile organisms. It is essential that these are suppressed, and in the past honey has always been boiled in order to sterilise it, and the boiling liquid skimmed in order to remove unwanted substances. In our view, this is an unfortunate way to treat a delicately flavoured substances, for volatile ingredients escape to the air and are lost to the subsequent mead or melomel. After the lengthy boiling recommended in many old recipes, the honey can scarcely be regarded as anything more than a source of invert sugar. There is one form of honey, namely heather honey, sometimes called ling honey, which can often benefit from moderate boiling and skimming, since this powerfully flavoured honey often contains more than the usual amount of bitter substances, but with the smaller amount of honey used in melomels, even this becomes unnecessary.

The most efficient way to sterilise honey is to make up the must of honey, fruit juice and other minor ingredients, then to sulphite it by adding 2 Campden tablets per 4.5 l (1 gal) (100 parts per million SO_2) and finally add the yeast starter 24 hours later in this way, none of the bouquet or flavouring power of the honey is lost and a much superior melomel is obtained.

At all times when making melomels great consideration should be given to the problem of conserving the delicate flavour and bouquet. Rackings in particular require care to ensure that no fruit pulp is sucked over into the second jar and that no splashing occurs. It is sometimes an advantage at the end of fermentation to sulphite the melomel with 2 Campden tablets per 4.5 l (1 gal) about a week before the melomel is racked. This has an effect similar to that of a fining agent because a great deal of yeast and other matter deposits itself to leave a clearer wine for racking.

Melomels, like other wines, benefit by maturing, but they can often be drunk as young as a few months with great satisfaction. Most melomels contain only about 10–12% alcohol by volume and reach their maximum maturity after about two years. There are many exceptions to this, however, as is the way with grape wines.

Some winemakers, particularly novices, will be tempted to make melomels of a higher alcoholic content than the range just quoted. This is often a mistake, as under these conditions the delicate balance of flavour between fruit juice and honey tends to be upset. It is better to make larger amounts and to drink it in larger glasses!

MELOMEL RECIPES
RECIPE No. 1 – APRICOT MELOMEL

Ingredients:

450 g (1 lb) Dried apricots	Nutrients
450 g (1 lb) Sultanas (or raisins)	Steinberg yeast
280 ml (½ pt) Elderflowers	Water to 4.5 litres (1 gal)
450 g (1 lb) Acacia blossom honey	15 g (½ oz) Malic acid

Method:

Dissolve the honey and nutrients in 4 l (7 pt) warm water. Add the apricots, chopped raisins or sultanas and 100 ppm sulphite (2 Campden tablets). After 24 hours, add the yeast starter and ferment on the pulp for 2–3 days. Strain off the latter and press lightly. Add the elderflowers 3 days later, ferment on the flowers for 2–3 days then strain off the latter. Make the volume up to 4.5 l (1 gal) with cold water and thereafter proceed as instructed in the basic procedure.

RECIPE No. 2 – BLACK MEAD

Ingredients:

1.8 kg (4 lb) Blackcurrants	Nutrients
280 ml (½ pt) Red grape concentrate	Bordeaux yeast
900 g (2 lb) English honey	10 g (¼ oz) Malic acid
(Light mixed flower)	Water to 4.5 litres (1 gal)

Method:

Dissolve the honey in 2 l (4 pt) warm water and add the acid and nutrients. Add the mixture to the crushed blackcurrants together with 1 l (2 pt) cold water and 100 ppm sulphite (2 Campden tablets). After 24 hours, add the yeast starter. Ferment on the pulp for 3 days then strain off the latter and press it lightly. Add the grape concentrate, make the volume up to 4.5 l (1 gal) with cold water (if necessary) and ferment until the gravity drops to just below 0. Rack at this stage, add 50 ppm sulphite (1 Campden tablet) and thereafter proceed as instructed in the basic procedure.

RECIPE No. 3 – CASK-MATURED MELOMEL

Ingredients:

11 kg (25 lb) Damsons	**Nutrients**
2.25 l (4 pt) Red grape concentrate	**Port or Madeira yeast**
1.5 l (2½ pt) Red rose petals	**Water to 22.5 l (5 gal)**
Heather honey as required	

Method:

Stone and crush the damsons. Dissolve 4.5 kg (10 lb) honey and nutrients in 13.5 l (3 gal) warm water and add to the damsons. Add 100 ppm sulphite (2 Campden tablets per 4.5 l (1 gal) and inoculate with the yeast starter 24 hours later. Ferment on the pulp for 2–3 days (check depth of colour periodically) then strain off the pulp and press it lightly. Add the grape concentrate and rose petals and ferment on the latter for 3 days before straining them off. Make the volume up to 22.5 l (5 gal) with cold water. Check the gravity and add 110 g (¼ lb) honey per 4.5 l (1 gal) every time the gravity drops to about 5 (rack off a little wine each time and dissolve the honey in this prior to its introduction). Any excess wine should be fermented separately and reserved for topping up purposes. Continue feeding the yeast in this manner until fermentation finally ceases, then rack the wine and thereafter proceed as directed in the basic procedure.

Notes:

(i) This wine requires fairly lengthy maturing. It should be matured in cask for about 2 years (hence the reason for giving a 22.5 l (5 gal) recipe) and in bottle for another 3 years at least and preferably longer.

(ii) Wild rose honey may be used instead of heather honey but the wine still requires long maturing.

(iii) The body of this wine may be increased by including 450 g (1 lb) bananas per 4.5 l (1 gal).

RECIPE No. 4 – CLOVER HONEY WINE

Ingredients:

2.25 l (½ gal) Clover flowers   ⅟₁₅th oz Tannin
570 ml (1 pt) White grape concentrate Nutrients
900 g (2 lb) Clover honey   Steinberg yeast
10 g (¼ oz) Malic acid   10 g (¼ oz) Tartaric acid
Water to 4.5 litres (1 gal)

Method:

Dissolve the honey, acid, tannin and nutrients in 3.5 l (6 pt) warm water then add another .5 l (1 pt) of cold water and 100 ppm sulphite (2 Campden tablets). After 24 hours add the yeast starter. Add the clover flowers 5 days after fermentation begins, ferment on the flowers for 2–3 days then strain them off. Make the volume up to 4.5 l (1 gal) with cold water if necessary and thereafter proceed as directed in the basic procedure.

RECIPE No. 5 – RED CURRANT MELOMEL

Ingredients:

2.25 kg (5 lb) Red currants   Nutrients
280 ml (½ pt) White grape concentrate Bordeaux yeast
900 g (2 lb) Guatemalan wild honey   Water to 4.5 litres (1 gal)

Method:

Dissolve the honey and nutrients in 3 l (5 pt) warm water and add the crushed red currants. Add 100 ppm sulphite (2 Campden tablets) and introduce the yeast starter 24 hours later. Ferment on the pulp for 2–3 days then strain it off and press lightly. Add the grape concentrate and make the volume up to 4.5 l (1 gal) with cold water. Ferment to dryness and thereafter continue as instructed in the basic procedure.

RECIPE No. 6 – GOOSEBERRY MELOMEL

Ingredients:

2.25 kg (5 lb) Green gooseberries   Yeast nutrients
450 g (1 lb) Sultanas   Steinberg yeast
675 g (1½ lb) Acacia blossom honey   Water to 4.5 litres (1 gal)
⅟₃₀th oz Tannin

Method:
Dissolve the honey in 3.5 l (6 pt) warm water and add the nutrients and tannin. Crush the gooseberries and sultanas and add to the honey solution. Add 100 ppm sulphite (2 Campden tablets) and leave for 24 hours before introducing the yeast starter. Ferment on the pulp for 3 days then strain off the pulp and press it lightly. Top up to 4.5 l (1 gal) with cold water and ferment to a gravity of about 0. Rack at this stage, add 50 ppm sulphite (1 Campden tablet) and thereafter continue as directed in the basic procedure.

RECIPE No. 7 – GOOSEBERRY MELOMEL

Ingredients:

2.7 kg (6 lb) gooseberries	**$\frac{1}{15}$th oz Tannin**
570 ml (1 pt) White grape concentrate	**Nutrients**
280 ml (½ pt) Yellow rose petals	**Sauternes yeast**
Acacia blossom honey as required	**Water to 4.5 litres (1 gal)**

Method:
Dissolve 900 g (2 lb) honey in 3.5 l (6 pt) water and add the tannin and nutrients. Crush the gooseberries and add to this the honey solution together with 100 ppm sulphite (2 Campden tablets). After 24 hours, add the yeast starter. Ferment on the pulp for 2–3 days then strain off the latter and press lightly. Add the grape concentrate and rose petals, ferment on the flowers for 2–3 days then strain off the latter. add the 110 g (¼ lb) honey per 4.5 l (gal) every time the gravity drops to 5 or less and continue doing so until fermentation finally ceases. Thereafter proceed as instructed in the basic procedure.

Note:
Recent experiments indicate that even better results can be obtained if the gooseberries have been allowed to become mouldy on the bush prior to picking. Gooseberries often split when very ripe and mould grows in the cracks. Such berries seem to produce better wine than perfect fruit, cf. Sauternes which is produced from grapes attacked by the mould Botrytis Cinerea.

RECIPE No. 8 – GRAPEFRUIT MELOMEL

Ingredients:

1 large can of Grapefruit juice	Yeast nutrients
1.2/1.3 l (43/46 fluid ounces)	15 g (½ oz) Tartaric acid
900 g (2 lb) Mixed wildflower honey	General purpose yeast

Method:

Dissolve the honey in 1.7 l (3 pt) water and add grapefruit juice, acid and nutrients. Sulphite 100 ppm (2 Campden tablets) and make volume up to 4.5 l (1 gal). After 24 hours introduce the yeast starter and ferment to dryness. Rack and sulphite 50 ppm (1 Campden tablet) and then continue as in basic procedure. Although this is a melomel, the characteristic "bite" of grapefruit flavour when blended with the honey is that of a well-balanced metheglin.

RECIPE No. 9 – LYCHEE MELOMEL

Ingredients:

450 g (1 lb) Canned lychees	Yeast nutrients
450 g (1 lb) Orange blossom honey	¹⁄₁₅th oz Tannin
450 g (1 lb) Sugar	Sauternes yeast
Water to 4.5 litres (1 gal)	10 g (¼ oz) Malic acid

Method:

Dissolve honey and sugar in 3.5 l (6 pt) water. Add lychees, nutrients, acid and tannin and make volume up to 4.5 l (1 gal). Add 100 ppm sulphite (2 Campden tablets). After 24 hours add yeast starter and ferment on the pulp for three days. Then strain off lychees and continue fermentation until completely dry. Rack, sulphite 50 ppm (1 Campden tablet) and continue as in basic procedure.

RECIPE No. 10 – ORANGE MELOMEL

Ingredients:

1 large can of Orange juice	Yeast nutrients
1.2/1.3 l (43/46 fluid ounces)	10 g (¼ oz) Tartaric acid
450 g (1 lb) Heather honey	¹⁄₁₅th oz Tannin
450 g (1 lb) Sugar	Bordeaux yeast

Method:
Dissolve the honey in 1.7 l (3 pt) water, add orange juice, tannin, acid, sugar and nutrients and make volume up to 4.5 l (1 gal). Sulphite 100 ppm (2 Campden tablets). After 24 hours add yeast starter and ferment to dryness. Rack and sulphite 50 ppm (1 Campden tablet) and thereafter continue as in basic procedure.

RECIPE No. 11 – ORANGE MELOMEL

Ingredients:

1.1 l (2 pt) Orange juice	**Nutrients**
1.3 kg (3 lb) Orange blossom honey	**Graves or Bordeaux yeast**
10 g (¼ oz) Malic acid	**¹⁄₁₅th oz Tannin**

Water to 4.5 litres (1 gal)

Method:
Extract the juice from sufficient oranges to provide 1.1 l (2 pt) juice. Dissolve the honey, malic acid, tannin and yeast nutrients in 2.25 l (4 pt) warm water and blend with the orange juice. Add 100 ppm sulphite (2 Campden tablets) and make the volume up to 4.5 l (1 gal) with cold water. After 24 hours, add the yeast starter. Ferment until the gravity drops to about 5 then rack. Rack again when the gravity drops to 0 and add 50 ppm sulphite (1 Campden tablet). Thereafter proceed as described in the basic procedure.

RECIPE No. 12 – PEACH MELOMEL

Ingredients:

2.7 kg (6 lb) Peaches	**¹⁄₃₀th oz Tannin**
330 ml (¾ pt) Elderflowers	**Nutrients**
(or 1 pkt dried flowers)	**Graves yeast**
1.1 kg (2½ lb) Acacia blossom honey	**10 g (¼ oz) Tartaric acid**
Water to 4.5 litres (1 gal)	**10 g (¼ oz) Malic acid**

Method:
Stone the peaches and press out the juice. Dissolve the honey in 2.25 l (4 pt) warm water and blend in the peach juice together with the acid, tannin and nutrients. Add 100 ppm sulphite (2 Campden tablets). After 24 hours, introduce the yeast starter and allow to

ferment for 7 days before adding the elderflowers. Ferment on the flowers for 3 days then strain them off and top up to 4.5 l (1 gal) with cold water. Allow to ferment until the gravity drops to 10, then rack it off the sediment. Rack again when the gravity drops to 5 and add 50 ppm sulphite (1 Campden tablet). Thereafter proceed as directed in the basic procedure.

RECIPE No. 13 – PINEAPPLE MELOMEL

Ingredients:

1.1 l (2 pt) Canned pineapple juice   Nutrients
280 ml (½ pt) White grape concentrate   Steinberg yeast
900 g (2 lb) Clover honey   Water to 4.5 litres (1 gal)
5 g (⅛ oz) Malic acid   5 g (⅛ oz) Tartaric acid
⅛₀th oz Tannin

Method:

Dissolve the honey, acid, tannin and nutrients in 2.25 l (4 pt) warm water, blend in the pineapple juice and grape concentrate and make up to 4.5 l (1 gal) with cold water. Add 100 ppm sulphite (2 Campden tablets) and after 24 hours introduce the yeast starter. Ferment until the gravity drops to 0, then rack and add 50 ppm sulphite (1 Campden tablet). Thereafter continue as directed in the basic procedure.

RECIPE No. 14 – PINEAPPLE MELOMEL

Ingredients:

1 large can Pineapple juice   ⅛₅th oz Tannin
1.2/1.3 l (about 43/46 fluid ounces)   10 g (¼ oz) Tartaric acid
900 g (2 lb) Lime blossom honey   Water to 4.5 litres (1 gal)
Yeast nutrients   Steinberg yeast

Method:

Dissolve the honey in 1.7 l (3 pt) water, add the pineapple juice, tannin, acid and nutrients. Sulphite 100 ppm (2 Campden tablets). After 24 hours make volume up to 4.5 l (1 gal) and introduce yeast starter. Ferment to dryness. Then rack, sulphite 50 ppm (1 Campden tablet) and continue as in basic procedure.

RECIPE No. 15 – RASPBERRY MELOMEL

Ingredients:

1.8 kg (4 lb) Raspberries	**Nutrients**
570 ml (1 pt) Red grape concentrate	**Port or Madeira yeast**
Lime blossom honey as required	**Water to 4.5 litres (1 gal)**

Method:

Dissolve 900 g (2 lb) honey in 3.5 l (6 pt) water. Add the nutrients, crushed raspberries, and 100 ppm sulphite (2 Campden tablets). After 24 hours, add the yeast starter and ferment on the pulp for 2–3 days. Strain off the pulp and press it lightly. Add the grape concentrate and make the volume up to 4.5 l (1 gal) with cold water if necessary. Add 110 g (¼ lb) honey per 4.5 l (1 gal) every time the gravity drops to 5 and repeat the procedure until fermentation finally ceases. Thereafter continue as directed in the basic procedure.

Collecting heather honey in Inverness.

Pyment, Hippocras, Metheglin and Cyser

Apart from mead and melomel, which have already been discussed, there are a number of other honey drinks which are worth making. All are of very ancient origin. Mead itself, being a scarce commodity, was reserved almost everywhere in the world for religious occasions. For general use and lesser celebrations, honey was generally mixed with some other fruit or herb. Across the whole Indo-Aryan world, for instance, a drink called Soma was made and when drunk in sufficient quantity, was believed to give strange and wonderful visions, and to ensure one's immortality. It appears to have been compounded from the yellow juice of some mountain plant, mixed with milk, barley meal and honey. Madhu, Haoma and Amrita were similar drinks, and from their great intoxicating power it would appear that in many cases some narcotic herb was included to enhance the effect of the alcohol produced and thereby create a form of hallucinatory drunkenness. These drinks are, however, beyond the scope of this book.

Pyment:

In Greek and Roman times, vineyards were planted and a fair quantity of wine was made. It was found that if honey were added to the juice from grapes, the must would ferment to a much higher alcoholic strength than by using the juice alone. These wines were called Pyments and were in fact the sweet dessert wines of those days. Although it is difficult to judge the strength of these wines, they probably did not contain more than about 15% alcohol because grapes at that time may have been less rich in sugar than nowadays due to less advanced viticulture and the yeast would not be able to attain a much higher strength. Only about 450–900 g (1 to 2 lb) of honey were added per 4.5 l (1 gal) of grape juice, but these Pyments nevertheless contained a great deal of residual sugar and would be rather too sweet for modern tastes.

Hippocras:

Hippocras, named after Hippocrates (the "Father of Medicine") was a typical product of Greek civilisation. Hippocrates himself was one of the great priest-physicians of his age, who made some attempt to codify medicine into a single science. As such, he investigated the properties of many herbs, and presumably used to add them to Pyment as a convenient method of storage and administration. Hippocras is thus a wine made from grape juice and honey, to which has been added herbs noted for their medicinal value or (subsequently) for their bouquet and flavour. In later centuries Hippocras, like Pyment, became a generic term for a whole series of spiced drinks both hot and cold.

Metheglin:

In our own country, the same process was at work, but having no great quantity of grape wine available the herbs were added to honey and fermented to a spiced mead called metheglin (from the Welsh word "Medclyglin" meaning "medicine"). All the valued herbs of the country were used – cloves, nutmeg, elderflowers, cowslips, rosemary and ginger together with a great many rarer ones compiled by the witches of the time. The quantities of herbs used were very large, and often an ounce each of six or seven herbs would be added to 4.5 l (1 gal) of mead or fermented in with it. In modern times, of course, herbs were added solely for flavour and the attempt was made to impart just enough spicy flavour to offset the cloying effects of the honey, bearing in mind the fact that their "dry" meads were often much sweeter than a dry mead of today. An extra sweet metheglin called sack metheglin was exported at one time, and as this drink was very high in alcohol, it is probable that some form of distillation was involved in its production.

One of the problems in making metheglin is that of obtaining a balanced flavour in the wine. When a metheglin has just finished fermenting, the herbs and the honey are both distinctly separate to the palate – almost fighting each other in fact – and a great deal of time is required for the wine to mature until the herb flavour has ameliorated and that of the honey almost disappeared entirely. The initial amount of herbs used, their variety and the type of honey all play a part in the process also, so that to make a good metheglin is a real winemaking achievement. By and large, metheglin is difficult to produce and also calls for a certain amount of luck if high quality is sought. For the Welsh patriot wishing to drink on St David's day, we would advise using a milder honey and a small amount of herbs only. It is always possible to increase the herbal flavour at any time during maturing simply by steeping some more herbs in the metheglin in a small muslin bag.

A second problem with metheglin (as also with Hippocras) is that of hazes caused by the herbs. These hazes can sometimes be cleared by fining with a proprietary fining such as Serena. They can, of course, be cleared by filtration, but this latter process is often most damaging to the bouquet and flavour of the metheglin and cannot be recommended.

Cyser:

When cyser was the staple drink of this country, someone, at some time, hit on the bright idea of adding honey to the apple juice, thereby obtaining a much stronger drink with an added exquisite flavour: This drink became known as Cyser. It was made mainly in the monasteries and abbeys, since the Church controlled most of the beehives, needing the wax for their candles, and in consequence Cyser seems to have declined when the monasteries lost their power and were dissolved.

It is a very worthwhile drink to make and follows the same basic principles as cider making, in that a mixture of cooking, cider and crab apples tends to produce a drink with more character than if dessert apples are used alone. Our friend Mr E. A. Roycroft tells us of one exception to this rule in that a splendid cyser can be made from James Grieves apples and honey, provided the apples used are *freshly picked from the tree.*

RECIPE No. 1 – PYMENT

Ingredients:

570 ml (1 pt) White grape concentrate   Yeast nutrients
900 g (2 lb) Clover honey   ¹⁄₁₅th oz Tannin
15 g (½ oz) Malic acid   Sauternes yeast
Water to 4.5 litres (1 gal)

Method:

Dissolve the honey in 3 l (5 pt) water, add the grape concentrate, acid, tannin, nutrients and sulphite 100 ppm (2 Campden tablets). After 24 hours add the yeast starter and make volume up to 4.5 l (1 gal). Ferment to dryness, rack carefully, add 50 ppm sulphite (1 Campden tablet) and thereafter continue as in basic procedure.

RECIPE No. 2 – PYMENT

Ingredients:

570 ml (1 pt) Red grape concentrate   Yeast nutrients
900 g (2 lb) Mixed wild flower honey   15 g (½ oz) Malic acid
Water to 4.5 litres (1 gal)   Bordeaux yeast

Method:

Dissolve the honey in 3 l (5 pt) water, add the grape concentrate, acid and nutrients and sulphite 100 ppm (2 Campden tablets). After 24 hours add the yeast starter and make up the volume to 4.5 l (1 gal) with water. Ferment to dryness, rack carefully, add 50 ppm sulphite (1 Campden tablet) and continue as directed in the basic procedure.

RECIPE No. 3 – HIPPOCRAS

Ingredients:

570 ml (1 pt) White grape concentrate   Yeast nutrients
900 g (2 lb) Heather honey   ¹⁄₁₅th oz Tannin
15 g (½ oz) Malic acid   10 g (¼ oz) Cinnamon
Water to 4.5 litres (1 gal)   General Purpose yeast

Method:
Dissolve the honey in 3 l (5 pt) water, add the grape concentrate, acid, tannin, nutrients and sulphite (2 Campden tablets). After 24 hours add the yeast starter and make up the volume to 4.5 l (1 gal) with water. When the gravity drops to about 5 rack and add the cinnamon. Rack again when the gravity drops to about 0, and add 50 ppm sulphite (1 Campden tablet). Thereafter proceed as in basic procedure.

RECIPE No. 4 – HIPPOCRAS

Ingredients:

570 ml (1 pt) Red grape concentrate	**Yeast nutrients**
900 g (2 lb) Heather honey	**Bordeaux yeast**
15 g (½ oz) Malic acid	**Peel of 1 small orange**
1 knob Root ginger	**(no pith) and juice**
4 Cloves	**Water to 4.5 litres (1 gal)**

Method:
Dissolve the honey in 2.25 l (4 pt) water. Boil the orange peel, ginger and cloves in 570 ml (1 pt) water for 15 minutes. Strain liquor over honey and add grape concentrate, nutrients and acid. Make up the volume to 4.5 l (1 gal) and sulphite 100 ppm (Campden tablets). After 24 hours add the yeast starter and ferment until gravity drops to about 15. Rack and sulphite 50 ppm (1 Campden tablet). Thereafter proceed as in basic procedure.

RECIPE No. 5 – METHEGLIN

Ingredients:

1.3 kg (3 lb) Heather honey Yeast nutrients
10 g (¼ oz) Tartaric acid **15 g (½ oz) Malic acid**
Steinberg yeast **Water to 4.5 litres (1 gal)**
Peel of 1 small lemon (no pith)
110 g (4 oz) Mixed herbs (any mixture of elderflowers, marjoram, cowslip, balm, mayblossom, mace according to availability)

Method:
Dissolve the honey in 3.5 l (6 pt) water. Add acid, lemon peel, herbs and nutrients and sulphite 100 ppm (2 Campden tablets).

After 24 hours add yeast starter. After 4 days strain off the herbs and peel and continue fermentation until gravity drops to 5 approximately. Rack and sulphite 50 ppm (1 Campden tablet) and continue as directed in basic procedure.

RECIPE No. 6 – METHEGLIN

Ingredients:

1.3 kg (3 lb) Clover honey   **Yeast nutrients**
10 g (¼ oz) Tartaric acid   **15 g (½ oz) Malic acid**
¹⁄₁₅th oz Tannin   **Zeltinger yeast**
Water to 4.5 litres (1 gal)   **1 pkt. Heath & Heather**
    dried flowers (cowslip,
    elderflower or coltsfoot)

Method:

Dissolve the honey in 3.5 l (6 pt) water. Add acid, tannin and nutrients. Sulphite 100 ppm (2 Campden tablets). After 24 hours add yeast starter. After 7 days fermentation add dried flowers and ferment on the pulp for 4 days, after which strain off the flowers and continue fermentation until the gravity drops to about 10. Rack and sulphite 50 ppm (1 Campden tablet). Thereafter continue as in basic procedure.

RECIPE No. 7 – CYSER VARIATION

Ingredients:

2.25 l (4 pt) Apple juice   **Nutrients**
280 ml (½ pt) White grape concentrate **Bordeaux yeast**
675 g (1½ lb) English honey   **Water to 4.5 litres (1 gal)**
15 g (½ oz) Mead acid mixture (equal parts tartaric and malic acids)

Method:

Dissolve the honey in 1.7 l (3 pt) warm water and blend in the apple juice, grape concentrate, acid and nutrients. Add 100 ppm sulphite (2 Campden tablets) and after 24 hours introduce the yeast starter. Make up the volume to 4.5 l (1 gal) with cold water, ferment until the gravity drops to 0, then rack. Thereafter proceed as directed in the basic procedure.

Other Honey Drinks

There are many mixed drinks under various names (Punch, Negus, Bishop, etc.) which use honey in fair quantities. Most of these are winter drinks, and reading through the works of Dickens, Dr Johnson and others one gets the impression that the main reason for fighting one's way through snow, highwaymen and biting winds was for that glorious moment when one arrived at an inn and was greeted by the round-faced jolly landlord with a great flaming bowl of bishop. The warmth of the inn, the hot drink circulating and the merry company, glad to be safe from the perils without, produced an experience which is hard to match today. Unfortunately, while little can be done to restore the past, a little imagination can, on occasion, recapture its memories. If, for instance, a Bishop has a little brandy to him so that he becomes well lit up and is carried flaming into a darkened room, an undoubted magic is added to the event, which thus will be remembered long afterwards.

The important thing with all mulled drinks is that they should be kept very hot but not boiling. If they boil, they soon lose their "kick" as the alcohol evaporates and is lost. By contrast, nothing is quite so depressing as a luke-warm drink of this sort. The second point to remember is that mulled drinks can be made as strong or as weak as you wish (alcoholically speaking) according to whether additions of spirits are made on the one hand or water on the other. A strong drink of this type will undoubtedly help to get a party going full-swing quickly if each guest is handed a steaming glass of bishop as he enters. On the other hand, many people have a mulled drink every night before retiring, and for this a more moderate strength is required.

Most mead-makers are also winemakers, and so will understand the type of wine required in the following recipes. A full-bodied sweet red wine is meant to substitute for the Port quoted in the original recipe. Similarly, a dry red wine is a substitute for Claret.

HONEY BISHOP

Take a large lemon, make about twelve incisions in it and insert cloves. Roast the lemon slowly in the oven. Put 570 ml (1 pt) of water 110 g (¼ lb) of honey and a pinch each of cinnamon, mace and allspice into a saucepan, bring to the boil and simmer gently until the volume has been reduced by half. Then, in another saucepan, bring to the boil a bottle of dry white wine. Put the roasted lemon and the contents of the two saucepans into a large punchbowl and add the juice of a lemon, a sprinkle of nutmeg and, if required, a dash of brandy. Serve while hot.

BRAGGOT

This drink, much valued in the 14th century in England, is very easily made. It represents a link between mead and ale. To make it, take 450 g (1 lb) malt extract, 450 g (1 lb) heather honey and 4 l (7 pt) of water and boil them together for 15 minutes, skimming the surface meanwhile. Add 10 g (¼ oz) citric acid and yeast nutrients, and when cool ferment with an ale yeast. When fermentation has finished, rack and mature for three months as though it were a wine. This drink is drunk from beer glasses or pewter tankards and is best served slightly chilled.

CAUDLE

In Shakespearian times, people were frequently "caudled" last thing at night with a great mug of hot honey beer. It presumably acted as a hot water bottle until you had drunk it, after which it warmed you within. Ladies in childbirth were also dosed liberally with it. It is made by pouring a quart of brown ale over a quarter of a pound of honey and a tablespoonful of ground oatmeal. This is then stood in front of the fire or placed in a low oven for a couple of hours, after which the beer is stirred, strained off and given a send-off with a pinch of nutmeg, the juice of a lemon and a glass of whisky or rum. It is marvellous for insomnia if a pint is drunk.

BOSWELL

Dr Johnson was a great compounder of Bishops, particularly after one of his jaunts with friends in the region of Covent Garden. In those days, if one were well-known in a tavern, one could make one's own Bishop, and he must have undoubtedly made the following one which was popular at the time. You can, if you wish, emulate Dr Johnson by drying the orange peel afterwards and grating it into a glass of port – he insisted it was good for indigestion and this may even be true!

Take a bottle of claret (or any dry red wine), a sliced orange, two tablespoonsful of honey, four cloves and a half a pint of water. Put these into a saucepan and bring to the boil (but only just). Add one wineglassful of Curaçao and one of brandy. Pour into glasses and grate a little nutmeg on top. A spoon should be placed in each glass to prevent breakage of the glass by heat.

ELDERBERRY NEGUS

In the early 18th century, a certain Colonel Francis Negus achieved fame for his family name by compounding a hot spiced port. Colonel Negus was at the time M.P. for Ipswich, and one night in the House of Commons when the temperature of the Chamber was very low and that of its members very heated (they were probably discussing whether Income Tax should be raised to the ruinous figure of 6d in the £), it occurred to him that if the port they were drinking were heated up and at the same time diluted with water, the members would feel better (being warmer) and their discussions become more temperate (as less alcohol per hour was absorbed). Since that time, countless Neguses have been made, so we make no apology in adding one of our own on behalf of amateur mead-makers.

Take a bottle of elderberry wine, half a pound of honey, six cloves and the pared rind and juice of a lemon together with 140 ml (¼ pt) of water. Heat these until almost boiling. Add a tot of brandy or rum and some grated nutmeg and serve while very hot.

YORKSHIRE NIGHTCAP

Another "just-before-bedtime" drink of the Middle Ages, whose name we have not been able to trace (hence one of our own) is made by bringing to the boil 570 ml (1 pt) of water, four level tablespoonsful of honey, four cloves and a half teaspoonful of allspice. In a separate saucepan, bring to the boil a quart of strong ale (Bass or Worthington) and when boiling blend the two together. Add a tot of brandy and a slice of lemon, and drink when cool enough.

CAPILLAIRE

At one time, Capillaire was an infusion of maidenhair fern, and later it was a Parisian spiced drink to which orange flower water had been added. As often happens with drinks of this type, a great many different recipes gradually evolved and the following seemed the simplest for most people to make. Into a wide-necked jar put 250 g (½ lb) of honey, 110 g (¼ lb) preserved ginger, 40 g (2 oz) candied lemon peel, the juice of 2 lemons and the peel of one of them and two wine glasses of redcurrant juice (Ribena will be satisfactory). Pour on 4.5 l (1 gal) of strong white wine, cover and leave for a month. Strain off the liquor and filter if necessary. Serve either chilled or warmed according to season.

MULLED HONEY WINE

Quite often winemakers might want to make a quick mulled wine but cannot be bothered with roasting lemons stuck with cloves and the like. The following recipe is streamlined to provide a satisfactory winter night's drink. Into a pan put one bottle of dry wine (white or red), 10 g (¼ oz) citric acid and a teaspoonful of whatever spice happens to be found in the kitchen (mace, cinnamon, allspice, ginger), plus a couple of cloves if available. Bring almost to the boil, and while heating add small amounts of honey until the taste is satisfactory. Serve immediately, if not already consumed during the tasting.

BOLTON ABBEY PUNCH

This is a drink for a hot summer's day, when the weary traveller can stop for a while amid the hum of the bees, tractors and passing cars. Mix together 2 tablespoonsful of honey, 2 tablespoonsful of lemon juice, half a bottle of gin and some crushed ice. The mixture can be chilled further in a refrigerator if necessary before serving.

LAMB'S WOOL

We cannot but marvel at recipes such as the following which we came across. Take 1½ kg (3 lb) of honey, 4 teaspoonsful of grated nutmeg, 40 g (2 oz) ginger and the juice of four lemons. Add 18 l (4 galls) of beer and heat until the herbs are well blended with the beer. Strain and serve immediately. (Presumably a friend or two dropped in!)

LAMB'S WOOL

An alternative recipe of great antiquity is more realistic these days than the preceding one. Take four large cooking apples and core them. Place them in a baking tin, fill the cored part with thick honey, sprinkle liberally with nutmeg and bake in a moderate oven for 45 minutes. Put the apples and liquor in a saucepan and pour on two quarts of brown ale. Heat gently, ladling the beer over the apples until enough flavour has been extracted, pour into a jug and serve immediately. The apples are normally eaten along with the drink.

PINEAPPLE HONEY PUNCH

Unlike the previous recipes, this is a modern one.
Empty a tin of pineapple chunks into a bowl. Meanwhile heat up two bottles of white wine until they start to boil. Pour over the pineapple and mix in 250 g (½ lb) of honey. Serve when cool enough to drink.

TWELFTH NIGHT WASSAIL

It was the usual custom, in former times, to make a powerful drink, float raisins on top and then set fire to the surface. Children would then play a game called "Snapdragon" in which they braved the flickering blue flames to rescue a wine-flavoured raisin for themselves. When the raisins had all been disposed of everyone gave a wassail (good health) toast to each other in the drink. Alas! Brandy was very cheap in those days. We give an alternative wassail bowl which, although from the 18th Century, is more economical than the earlier version.

Boil together 570 ml (1 pt) water, 1 cup of honey, 4 cloves and 3 sticks of cinnamon for five minutes. Add two lemons thinly sliced and allow to stand for 7 or 8 minutes. Add a bottle of medium-dry red wine and heat slowly until just below boiling point. Pour into a jug and serve very hot.

WINTER WARMER

This Negus has the advantage that it is made by the glass. It is a very warming drink, low in alcohol and as such could be given even to children without risk (older children naturally, who want to join in their parents' merry-making).

Take a glass of Port or similar type wine and put it into a long glass. Add a teaspoonful of honey and a slice of lemon and fill up the glass with boiling water. Stir well, and remove lemon slice before drinking.

"BISHOP" MATHEWS BISHOP

In 1832, William Hone in his Year Book describes Bishop as a delicious winter beverage of antiquity beyond the memory of man, and he quotes this little rhyme by the editor of a University magazine *Oxford Nightcaps:*

"Three cups of this prudent man may take;
The first of these for constitution's sake,
The second to the lass he loves the best,
The third and last to lull him to his rest."

In London, they made Bishops with oranges rather than lemons. It was said that none knew better how to make a Bishop than the father of Mathews, the great comedian of the 1830's, so we give his recipe:

Make incisions in the rind of an orange and stick them with cloves and roast the orange by the fire. Put small but equal quantities of cinnamon, cloves, mace, allspice and a knob of ginger into a saucepan with 285 ml (½ pt) of water. Boil it until it be reduced by half. Meanwhile boil a bottle of port wine, and, by applying a lighted taper to the pan burn out a portion of the spirit from it. Add the roasted orange and spice unto the wine and let it stand by the fire for ten minutes. Rub some knobs of sugar on the rind of an orange and add them to the mixture along with the juice of an orange (not roasted). Grate in nutmeg and sweeten to your taste with honey and you have a Bishop.

If a dry red wine like claret is used it is called a "Cardinal" while if champagne is used it is known as a "Pope". There is also another member of the Bishop family known as "Lawn Sleeves" which is made exactly as a Bishop except that madeira or sherry is substituted for port and three glasses of hot calves-foot jelly are added.

INDEX

Other titles in the Amateur Winemaker Series

AMATEUR WINEMAKER RECIPES (Edited by C.J.J. BERRY)
Recipes from the monthly magazine, 'Amateur Winemaker'. Over 200 are gathered together here in one vital reference.

BETTER COUNTRY WINES (P.W. TOMBS)
A comprehensive, down-to-earth book which not only describes successful wines but advises what to avoid and how to prevent or cure disorders in winemaking. Includes over 100 recipes plus suggestions for experiment and variation.

BETTER WINES FROM CONCENTRATES (T. EDWIN BELT)
This remarkable book includes day-by-day detailed instructions on processing and over 300 recipes for all types of wine, punches, cups and coolers, cordials, cocktails, vermouths, liqueurs etc., with additional information on serving, wine and cheese, even tobacco fermenting.

GREAT FERMENTATIONS (MARION WHITTOW)
Marion Whittow relates her winemaking experience on this useful and amusing book. Her advice on the home winemaking process is full of commonsense and her witty cartoons enliven the text.

HOW TO MAKE WINES WITH A SPARKLE
(JOHN RESTALL and DON HOBBS)
Discover the secrets of producing champagne-like wine of superb quality. The natural choice for celebrations and festive occasions, sparkling wines have a place in everybody's winery, and now the amateur winemaker who follows this book's methods can produce them for himself.

100 WINEMAKING PROBLEMS ANSWERED (CEDRIC AUSTIN)
Cedric Austin answers a selection of questions put to him over the years on the most frequent problems encountered by amateur winemakers.

130 NEW WINEMAKING RECIPES (C.J.J. BERRY)
Contains tests and reliable recipes, many of which are unique to this publication, but certain well-tried favourites are also included.

MAKING WINES LIKE THOSE YOU BUY
(BRYAN ACTON and PETER DUNCAN)
How to reproduce the flavour and quality of commercial wines in your own home. Sauternes, hocks, Madeiras and champagne are all possibilities with the help of this book.

MODERN WINEMAKING TECHNIQUES (GLADYS BLACKLOCK)
Explains clearly and concisely how to obtain the best results from a wide range of ingredients.

PROGRESSIVE WINEMAKING
(PETER DUNCAN and BRYAN ACTON)
This book is the outcome of many years practical experience of winemaking at home, and its whole emphasis is upon producing quality wines which will bear full comparison with the popular wines of the Continent. It shows clearly the path to advanced winemaking, and consequently will be warmly welcomed by those who already know something of the subject, but it will also prove invaluable to the complete beginner, for whom typical recipes have been included. Every aspect of winemaking is covered thoroughly.

RECIPES FOR PRIZEWINNING WINES (BRYAN ACTON)
Nearly all these recipes have won prizes at national and regional shows and the amateur who follows them carefully will produce high quality wines with the minimum of effort and the maximum of certainty.

SCIENTIFIC WINEMAKING – MADE EASY
(J.R. MITCHELL and T. TIMBRELL)
The author was a quality control executive at one of the largest British beverage firms, and thus ideally qualified to write such a book. 2nd edition in preparation, due March 1987.

THE WINEMAKER'S DICTIONARY (PETER McCALL)
A comprehensive A-Z of the art and science of winemaking from the preparation of the ingredients to decanting the resultant wine. Thorough cross-referencing and a systematic approach make this an indispensible reference book for all winemakers.

WINEMAKER'S COMPANION (C.J.J. BERRY and BEN TURNER)
This book gives a sensible and practical explanation of what modern winemaking is all about, and describes the basic principles, main ingredients, equipment required, and processes for making wines and beers of good quality. It deals in detail with the making of an individual wine and gives recipes for many more, using fruit and certain other ingredients which the authors have found to be successful. Subjects also dealt with are cellarcraft, the serving and appreciation of wine, keeping records and how to take part in competitions. As well as covering every aspect of the hobby, this also makes an excellent reference book.

WINEMAKING SIMPLIFIED (E.H. CORNISH)
Designed to encourage the beginner rather than blind him with science, this book uses one man's practical experience to give guidance to successful winemaking.

WINEMAKING WITH CANNED & DRIED FRUIT (C.J.J. BERRY)
Easy, clean and economical, this simple system of winemaking will appeal to everyone. This book tells how to make delightful wines from low-price ingredients from markets, grocers and chemists.

WINEMAKING WITH CONCENTRATES (PETER DUNCAN)
Invaluable to the flat dweller who enjoys wine but lacks the facilities to make it from grapes and other fruits, and to any winemaker who uses concentrates.

WINEMAKING WITH ELDERBERRIES (T. EDWIN BELT)
Elderberry wine is a great favourite, with the fruit available for anyone to gather from the countryside. Describes the different varieties of fruit and ways to make the best of them.

WORLDWIDE WINEMAKING RECIPES (ROY EKINS)
This intriguing book gives dozens of original recipes for unusual wines – Ugli, Dingleberry and many more.

ALL ABOUT BEER & HOME BREWING (BOB PRITCHARD)
Bob Pritchard has spent his working life in the brewing trade and was in at the start of the homebrewing boom when it took off in the 60s. His vast knowledge and experience are condensed into this book.

BEER KITS AND BREWING (DAVE LINE)
All the latest information on beer kits, hopped worts, malt extract and the new equipment is here, set out clearly in a manner which will appeal to the beginner and enthusiast alike.

THE BIG BOOK OF BREWING (DAVE LINE)
This definitive handbook covers every aspect of homebrewing. Traditional techniques used to brew the finest beers and ales are adapted for the amateur and described with authority and humour.

BREWER'S DICTIONARY (PETER D. McCALL)
This book has around 1300 entries covering all apects of brewing and giving explanations on technical terms and different beer types. Ingredients for brewing are dealt with in detail, for example there are 79 entries covering the necessary information on hops. Everything is clearly presented in alphabetical order and extensive cross referencing leads the reader to related topics.

BREWING BEERS LIKE THOSE YOU BUY (DAVE LINE)
There's a good chance you'll find your favourite brew here – now you can learn how to brew it at home at a fraction of the pub cost! Recipes have been extracted from information given by the breweries themselves about their beers.

BREWING BETTER BEERS (KEN SHALES)
The complete guide for the advanced enthusiast. All the recipes have been repeatedly tested and can be relied on to produce beers of superb quality, true to type.

BREWING LAGER (J. ALEXANDER)
This is the only book which deals solely with larger brewing and covers every stage in detail. There is an explanation of the various types of lager and the necessary ingredients, with details on refridgeration, bottling and casking methods. The beginner is taken step by step through the first brew onto making genuine continental lager. A number of recipes, suitable for the beginner and the experienced brewer, are also included.

THE HAPPY BREWER (WILF NEWSOM)
The home brewer who wishes to go more deeply into the theory and techniques of brewing will find all the answers in this book.

HINTS ON HOME BREWING (C.J.J. BERRY)
Provides step-by-step instruction on various methods and guides the amateur in selection of equipment and ingredients. 150,000 copies sold.

HOME BREWED BEERS AND STOUTS (C.J.J. BERRY)
The first modern book on home brewing, this was an instant success when it was first published in 1963. This latest edition contains up-to-date information on how to brew fine beers and stouts of authentic flavour and strength for as little as 6p a pint! Send S.A.E. for our current price list.

HOME BREWING FOR AMERICANS (DAVID MILLER)
Here are simple ways to brew all kinds of beers from American malts. Fifteen fully detailed recipes through Light to Dark Lagers, Ales and Bitters, Porter and Stout.

BE A WINE AND BEER JUDGE (S.W. ANDREWS)
The author was the founder chairman of the Amateur Winemakers National Guild of Judges. In his book he advises the proficient amateur on the right steps to take to qualify as an officially recognised wine judge.

SUGAR-FREE WINES AND BEERS (PETER D. McCALL)
With an increasing concern about diet and heatlh, this book has been written to enable winemakers and brewers to produce sugar-free wines and beers. It covers aspects of health related to wine and beer making and has an extensive section on diabetes.

GROWING VINES (NICK POULTER)
Down to earth advice, a guide to vine varieties and a 'through the year' diary are all there to help the enthusiast succeeded in this exciting new venture.

MAKING CIDER (JO DEAL)
Describes how, with the minimum of equipment, a glut of apples can be converted into delicious cider for drinking and culinary use.

MAKING INEXPENSIVE LIQUEURS (REN BELLIS)
The gamut of exotic liqueurs is described, then the reader is initiated into how to reproduce these flavours and textures for himself.

MAKING MEAD (BRYAN ACTON and PETER DUNCAN)
This is an informative and entertaining guide to one of the world's oldest crafts. It combines ancient and modern techniques to give today's reader the complete mead-making picture.

VINES IN YOUR GARDEN (JAMES PAGE-ROBERTS)
This is the book for those with a little garden space who wish to make their own wine and eat their own grapes. The author's clear, step-by-step approach is complemented by his explanatory diagrams and illustrations by Bernard Venables.

WINES FROM YOUR VINES (NICK POULTER)
The sequel to 'Growing Vines', this book goes on to help the viticulturist make the most of his harvest by setting out in a detailed and practical way instructions on all aspects of winemaking from grapes.

WOODWORK FOR WINEMAKERS (C.J. DART and D.A. SMITH)
The authors combine their knowledge of woodworking and wine-making to show the amateur winemaker how to build his own equipment. Be it a winepress, fruit pulper or winery, the instructions are all here, with clear, detailed working drawings to help you succeed.

FIRST STEPS IN WINEMAKING (C.J.J.BERRY)
Universally known as 'the Winemaker's Bible', this book is an inspiration to beginners in winemaking. It covers terminology, basic facts and techniques and also gives an invaluable month by month guide to seasonal recipes for wine. There is also advice on the social side of the hobby – wine circles and competitions.